GODIVA F___ TO

A

BACKBEAT

A PICTORIAL JOURNEY THROUGH
COVENTRY & WARWICKSHIRE MUSIC
1960's-1980's

Pete Chambers

Keep Rockin'

Peter Ch...

Foreword by Bob Brolly MBE

When asked to write this foreword, I was truly honoured. I have known Pete for a long time and, like many people, know him as Coventry's very own 'Mr Music Man'. His knowledge of the Coventry and Warwickshire music scene is legendary, and in this book, he shares his memories in words and pictures, some of which may embarrass a few people, including my band Calvary – see bouffants inside.

Over the years, Coventry & Warwickshire has had a lot to offer music-wise, from Vince Hill, Frank Ifield and Two Tone to the stars of today, the fabulous young band, The Enemy, and of course, all other wonderful acts in between.

Many of the people featured in this book, I have probably met during my radio programme on BBC Coventry & Warwickshire. Every Friday, Pete and I go 'Backtracking' - just an excuse for a couple of old boys to reminisce.

This is Pete's 4th book exploring the local music scene, this time with the emphasis on pictures, each one being a moment frozen in time forever. Sadly, some of the faces are no longer with us, they have moved on to a much better place.

Yes, it is great to see all these old pictures of everyone, if only to remind me I am not the only one who looked a right eejit in the good old days.

Thank you Pete for asking me to write this foreword, and of course, for yet another gem of a book.

Bob Brolly, August, 2007

Introduction

Hello music fans, welcome to Godiva Rocks With a Backbeat. What we have here is a bit of a hybrid, many people have asked for a reprint of my first book Godiva Rocks. While others have requested a book of the best of my Coventry Telegraph Backbeat columns. So I have combined the two and come up with a book that will hopefully have combined appeal.

This publication is really all about photographs, I have amassed many of them over the years, and although Godiva Rocks included pictures, most of them lacked any great detail because of their size. This time they dominate the pages, and information on each entry is included in three text boxes. This is not intended as a definitive guide, the entries were decided purely on the availability of photographs in my collection, or those that were given to me by the artists. Sorry to the bands and artist that didn't make it, nothing personal.

- A white text box contains the name of the artist, where they hail from, and a small amount of information on each one, as much as you would get from a photographic caption.
- Grey text boxes include quotes from the artist, and are usually sourced from my Backbeat columns.
- Black text boxes contain trivia of that particular artist and are usually sourced from my Backbeat columns.

Some of the photos in this book have been published in Backbeat, some I have never published before. Entries are listed in their various decades, other than that entries are not in any particular order.

Coventry and Warwickshire has always had a huge amount of musical talent, most of these are represented here. The story finishes book-wise in 1989, obviously it continued and indeed still continues with the current success of our latest star bands The Enemy and the Ripps.

May it never stop, keep on a rockin'.......

Pete Chambers, August, 2007

WITH THANKS TO..........

Big thanks to all the bands and artists featured in this book, for their quotes, photographs, information and of course their rockin' good music.

Much appreciation and thanks to all our advertisers.

Also huge thanks to; My wife Julie, Bob Brolly, Kev Monks, Arl & Carol Grove, Neol Davies, Phil Daniel, Jerry Dammers, Horace Panter, Steve & Heather Taylor, Ken & Libby at Antony Rowe, Vince Holliday, CV One, Roger Vaughan, Coventry City Council, Hannah Tobin, Rich Elms Alan Kirby, John West and the Coventry Telegraph.

ISBN –13 978-0-9544125-5-5
ISBN-10 0-9544125-5-9
EAN 9780954412555

This book is dedicated to the memory of
Dave 'Biffo' Beech,
1945 - 2007.
A great drummer and wonderful human being,
paradidling in paradise.

Contents

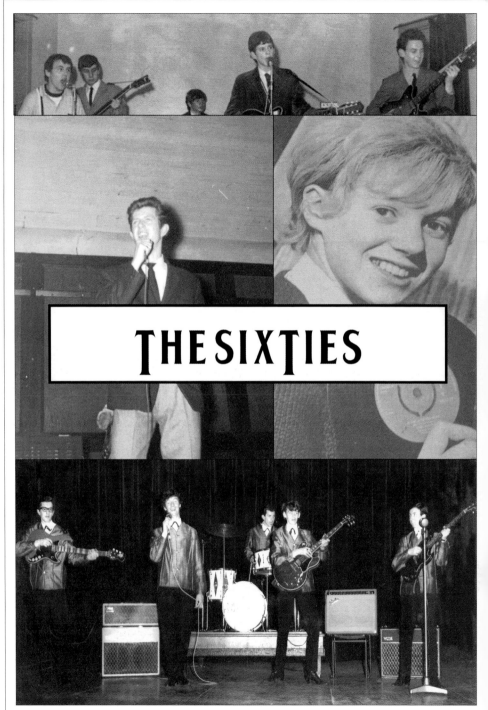

THE SIXTIES

The Chuckles
Nuneaton
Formed in Nuneaton in 1960, they became the backing band for the legendary Gene Vincent for a short while.

Photo above- George Beardmore (Lead Guitar), Len Bayly (Bass Guitar) Dave Dyde (Drums) and Barry Spruce (Organ)

"Our Birmingham Agent was seeking a typical rock group to back no other than the legendary Gene Vincent who was on a UK tour at the time. (He was having problems with his standard backing group for the northern part of the tour) so Alan our manager said we were the guys that could make up the short fall and consequently were asked to appear at the Midland Hotel in Birmingham the next day for an interview, we all hit it off and got the gig". **Len Bayly**

Gene had promised more dates in the future including London, but in the meantime Len and Dave had become apprentices at the then Rootes Motor Company and had committed hundred percent to their work careers. So it never happened again.

John Harris once tuned John Lennon's Rickenbacker guitar for him at The Matrix Ballroom in Coventry, November 1962.

"We played every Friday evening and we did 35 weeks residency there, I recall that there was four people there on the first night, but by the time we got to night 35 the place was heaving. There wasn't even any space to step-down from the stage" **John Harris.**

The Countdowns
Leamington Spa
The band was formed in February 1963 when friends Bob Wilson (bass) and Gary Mayo (drums) (who had played in a skiffle band in the army together) recruited Ken Smith in on rhythm guitar. The last piece in the jigsaw was lead guitarist John Harris, who was recruited via an advert in the Coventry Evening Telegraph. Photos- above, John Harris 2006, top and bottom-the Countdowns.

Sam Spade and the Gravediggers
Rugby
R 'n' B band that came out of the Phantom 5, Sam Spade's real name was Ray Barrett. They were hard working, playing all over the area but split in 1966 and some members became the Tea Set. Photos– Both promo pics.

"I remember playing with Coventry's Sorrows and being shocked seeing guitarist Pip Witcher using his Stratocaster as a dartboard, and travelling down to Soho's famous 2i's club to audition for Promoter Larry Parnes and then backing recording star Danny Rivers. Sadly we never recorded ourselves and split after "Sam" finally decided to call it a day in 1966". **Andy Hayward**

A typical set would include Smokestack Lightening, Hoochie Coochie man and Walking The Dog. We were dubbed R'n'B Kings of The Midlands by the local press and we were immortalised in Alan Clayson's book about 60's pop groups entitled Beat Merchants,.

11

Janet and the Three Spires
Coventry

Although they became based in Bedworth and Nuneaton they called themselves Janet and The Three Spires because of their connections with Coventry where they all originally came from. From October 63 to April 64 a time span of just six months they had an amazing 38 bookings.

Photos– Bottom of page-Jean and the Three Spires, right Keith on drums

Keith was once asked to join the illustrious Ken Platt and his golden trumpet after he had played drums for him. Keith turned down the offer of cruise line work, bad move as four months later he was to leave Janet and The Three Spires anyway.

"One of the most memorable gigs was at The Tollbar in Coventry, We were playing to an all male audience", Keith says, "they absolutely loved us, when we came out though it got really frightening, they mobbed our van, banging on the roof and windows and nearly tipped it over. For a moment we knew how the Beatles felt, and what it was like to be that popular". **Keith Frost**

Johnny B Great and the Goodmen
Coventry
Part of the Larry Page stable, based at The Orchid Ballroom in Coventry. They released a string of great Decca singles including the superb Acapulco 1922. Front man Johnny Goodison went on to find fame as part of the original Brotherhood of Man and as a songwriter/producer.

Photos- main photo Johnny and the boys outside The Orchid in Coventry, left Nigel Lomas in 2004, and below Johnny circa Acapulco 1922.

The Goodmen and Rolling Stones were both banned from Knutsford Services, after a well-tempered sugar cube fight broke out between the two groups in the cafe.

The Goodmen were a gnat's whisker away in securing the session, but because they had just had a single out, the song "Do You Love Me" was given to Brian Poole and The Tremeloes instead. Frustratingly for Johnny and the boys it went straight to number one. Nigel remembers another similar 'oh so near' experience. "We were set to appear in a film, but once again fate was not kind and our transport broke down. Johnny went on ahead while we waited for the van to be fixed by the time we made it to the studio Johnny had already performed "If I had A Hammer" on his own. Our moment of film glory had gone". **Nigel Lomas**

The Tea Set
Rugby

Andy Hayward, Bob Bostrum and Geoff Anthill formed the Tea Set from the remnants of Sam Spade and the Gravediggers with the introduction of guitarist Andy Kerrigan and vocalist 'Little' Joe Conway from Ireland's Miami Showband. Photo-a rare shot of the Tea Set

"We were kitted out in custom-made outfits playing hard rock", Andy admits, "We worked for entrepreneur Reg Calvert-he of Radio London and Fortunes fame. We stood in for stable mates "Pinkertons Assorted Colours" after they went off touring with their hit "Mirror, Mirror" and took over their Nags Head residency in Nuneaton. **Andy Hayward**

They were probably best remembered as the band on stage at Nuneaton's Co-op Hall when 4 people were tragically crushed to death on a staircase attempting to get into a packed New Year's Eve ball.

The Tea Set once had their power turned off at a gig in Coventry's Central Hall, when a janitor who had obviously never seen stage pyrotechnics attempted to put out the bands special effects with a fire extinguisher!

THE ORCHID BALLROOM

FRIARS PROMOTIONS present for

COVENTRY CITY FOOTBALL CLUB

on Friday, 25th October, 1963

8.0 P.M—1.0 A.M.

THE "SKY BLUE" TWANG

The Dance of the Year *for the* Team of the Year

WITH

TONY MARTIN and the ECKO FOUR

THE FEARLESS AVENGERS

THE MATADORS AND THE UNKNOWNS

We have the THREE TOP COVENTRY GROUPS and this new Mystery Group introduced by FRIARS for the first time ever

---

A £5 Prize for "Miss Sky Blue"

An "Off the Cuff" Beauty Challenge

AND LOTS OF FUN WITH

"Wee Georgie on the Ball"

The whole Show compered by that irrepressible character

JONNIE MEDLOCK

— TICKETS ARE NOW ON SALE EVERYWHERE —

From JILL HANSON'S, THE ORCHID BALLROOM, THE BANTAMS' FIGHTING FUND STAFF, THE "QUIK CHIC" AND ANYWHERE YOU SEE A FRIARS PROMOTION

ASK THE STAFF OR GROUPS PLAYING

Come along and give a great Kick Off to the first Dance organised for a Great Team

"LET'S ALL TWANG TOGETHER"

FRIARS PROMOTIONS, 34 HEATH ROAD, COVENTRY
or Telephone BEDWORTH 2203

What's this we hear? A "Scrum Down" Twang?

Printed by Franklin & Gates, 272 Windmill Road, Coventry

A flyer for one of the areas famous Twang Dances. The word 'Twang' had nothing to do with guitars or suspenders, it was a nondescript word like 'thingy' or 'whatchamacallit'. Mick Teirnan of Friars Promotions came up with the name. Whatever it meant 'Twangs' were a great success and pulled in the punters.

"Earlier that year Geoff Timms had bought an old Bedford van (every group had to have a van) which was supposed to ferry us to and from gigs but it was a bit of a 'banger' and at least once we arrived late at a booking after pushing the lifeless jalopy uphill. By today's standards it would not have been allowed on the road. I had finished school by then and some non-band friends ask me to join them on a short camping holiday in Cornwall. On the spur of the moment I decide to go. The band had been thinking of approaching a girl we knew who we'd thought might make a good lead singer in the band and whilst I'm away Ned and Geoff decide to drive over to see her and discuss it. Together they set off towards Hampton In Arden on 10th August 1967 and just outside Balsall Common they crash head-on into a lorry and both were killed outright. Ned was 18 and Geoff 19. If I hadn't decided to go to Cornwall on a whim I would have been with Ned and Geoff. There but for fortune. ". **John Green**

The Trane supported Jeff Beck in Rugby in 1967. The band included Jeff Beck, Ronnie Wood on bass, Rod Stewart on vocals and (bizarrely) Graham Edge from the Moody Blues on drums. More information on The Trane can be found at www.skylinesongs.com

The Trane
Kenilworth
Formed in 1966, they called themselves "The 'Trane" after John Coltrane the jazz saxophonist, emulating the Yardbirds who took their name from the sobriquet of another jazz saxophonist, Charlie Parker".

Photo-- Nigel Maltby, Laurie French, Geoff Timms, John Green & Ned Foyle.

The Liberators
Rugby
They recorded a single 'It Hurts So Much' under Shel Talmy and engineered by Glyn Johns with Jimmy Page on extra guitar. It was done at IBC Portland Place, the B side was entitled 'You Look So Fine'".
Photos-studio and live shots.

In November 1965 The Liberators under the guidance of Reg Calvert became Pinkerton's Assorted Colours and scored the massive hit Mirror, Mirror.

"We had to do a session with (Coventry born) Tony Clarke from Decca. It was easier for him to come up to us on the train, so we rang round for a hall, nowhere was free. We rang Bilton, they said sorry we're all set out for a jumble sale. I asked, is the stage empty? That's all we need, and only for 2 hours. They said OK as long as we didn't touch anything in the hall. So we got set up on this stage with the curtains closed and Tony Clarke came along and brought Jimmy Page with him. Jimmy Page picked out a couple of kerosene bicycle lamps out of the jumble and left Ten Shillings for them. That was a fortune then and the jumblers were more than happy with that. But Jim was no fool, I soon learned that the lamps were worth about £5 down the Portobello market!" **Tom Long**

The Little Darlings
Coventry
Formed in the early 60's, they released the R'n'B influenced single 'Little Bit O'soul', but it failed to chart. They became The Sensations in 1967.

Photos-Below John Gilroy, then and now, and the Darlings hug a tree.

"When we played our single live at the Locarno", says-John, "I played the keyboard fills on my guitar, someone said that it sounded better live, than on record, boy we were sick! The single (released on the Fontana Record label), was written by Ivy League members John Carter and Ken Lewis. The Disc music paper said of it...."The Little Darlings' noise sounds just great". **John Gilroy**

Little Bit O'soul may have failed to chart for the Little Darlings, but the song was later recorded by the American band from Ohio The Music Explosion and made number two in the US charts in 1967. That wasn't the end of the song by any means. In 1983 punk godfathers The Ramones covered the song on their Subterranean Jungle album, and gave it a new lease of life.

18

Jeff Lynne was once a member of the band (for a short spell). He left the band and joined the Birmingham unit the Nightriders, who became the Idle Race. Then onto The Move, ELO and world domination.

The Mad Classix
Coventry
Known for their 'mad' on stage antics, they played six months in Germany, and even recorded a single Hunny Bunny. Bev Jones was once a member and married lead vocalist Johnny Wells.
Photos– right with Bev, above in Coventry, below reunion time 2005!

"I wouldn't have missed the German tour for the world, and it was hard for me because I had a wife and family at home. We worked three to four hours a night six days a week and rehearsed on the seventh. Yes it was hard work, but an opportunity I couldn't miss". **Ron Smith**

19

The Matadors
Hinckley

The Matadors played so much in Coventry that most people thought they were from the town, indeed they once won a Best Coventry Band contest. They recorded one single for Colombia, A Man's Gotta Stand Tall (as the Four Matadors) produced by none other that the legendary Joe Meek.

Photos– Below at Coventry Cathedral, bottom left Dave and Harry and that single 2006, bottom right the band in their 'Fearless Matadors' stage.

"We went down to Holloway Road, London, to the house Joe Meek used as his recording studio. I found him arrogant and not over-friendly, instead of a normal mixing desk Meek had his in a stack and worked standing up, and he looked like a teddy boy. He fixed Dan Findley's piano keys with paper and drawing pins to get the sound he wanted, everything was very experimental". **Dave Colkin**

Their Colombia single A Man's Gotta Stand Tall/Fast Cars and Money is now worth around £80 in mint condition, thanks mainly for it's Joe Meek connection.

The Mustangs
Kenilworth

Kenilworth's big rock n roll band of the early 60's. Lynn Curtis fronted the band for a time as did Ricky Starr (bottom left) with his unfeasibly large DA haircut. Lynn went on to release the country-influenced Decca 45 "House for Sale".

Photos– below Lynn Curtis in the 60's and Pat Brook as he is today

The Mustangs were one of the first ever bands to use echo effect. Martin Noble borrowed his Dad's Telefunken reel-to-reel tape recorder and inserted a switch that made it play back within a spit second, - instant echo!! (Just a single one, we weren't greedy!) It sounded great to us although we knew we couldn't play for more than 45 minutes as the tape would run out!

"Our parents all realised we were serious about the band and agreed to stand guarantors for a brand new set of guitars. We decided that Fenders were old hat and American. – Burns, however were English and played by the Shadows! (big mistake) They were certainly well made and finished. We also invested in a Vox AC 30 amp and speaker cabinet. We were beginning to look like a band now, with our plain white shirts and jeans. We then met a character called Vince Martin from Coventry who was at the tail end of a singing career but could still make Ricky Starr look second rate, especially in his gold lame suit! Vince did a few gigs with us and livened up the band no end! I remember going all the way to a Skegness holiday camp in his Mini Traveller with most of our gear on board!" **Pat Brook**

New City Sounds
Coventry
The New City Sounds, who came to fame as two times winners of the hit TV show Opportunity Knocks! Coming together in 1969 at the old West End Club (now the HQ of Mercia FM), led by Frank Dempsey the band became a permanent fixture at the Free and Easy weekends.

Photos– below right NCS with Frank on the left, insert Tony Pyatt and Arthur Griffith in 2005, below the new NCS with Tony in the line-up (with trumpet).

Band leader Frank Dempsey is the father of local folk legend Kevin Dempsey.

The song they won Opportunity Knocks with was "Stop the World and Let me Off" it was recorded at Midland Sound Recorders in Balsall Common.

I" Came in at the deep end, I was petrified, one minute I was in this small time band The Monroes the next I was playing in front of packed audiences with Opportunity Knocks Winners, it was unreal".
Tony Pyatt

22

The Orchids
Coventry

The Orchids comprised of three 15 year old school girls (Georgina Oliver, Pamela Jarman and Valerie Jones), managed by Larry Page. They signed to Decca releasing a series of excellent singles including the 'almost a hit' Love Hit Me. Though the groups tour de force was Solider Boy written by Georgina herself.

Photos-Top the Orchids as they were, bottom the image change, inserts Georgina and Val as they look today.

The Orchids are featured on the following CD compilations, Go Girl-Dream Babes Vol.4 (Love Hit Me, Mr Scrooge and Gonna Make Him Mine) and the recently re-released The Girls Scene (Oo-Chang-A-lang and Soldier Boy).

"We were once taken out to lunch by Andrew Oldham (Stone's manager) We were so in awe of him I don't think we uttered a word to him the whole time we were out. He took us to a posh pavement cafe in Soho. We didn't know whether he was paying or not and as we didn't have any money (we were still on pocket money and saw virtually no money from our record sales) we said we weren't hungry (we were!) and had nothing to eat! He must have thought we were totally weird".
Georgina Oliver

Pam   George   Val

Sue & Mary
Coventry

Two 13-year-old Cardinal Wisemen schoolgirls who were overheard by their teacher singing a song in the playground that turned out to be written by the girls. They signed to Decca Records in 1965 and released the self-penned single "Traitor In Disguise"!, and the B-Side,"I Love You (Yes I Do)".

Photos– Below the girls at school, bottom my prized demo copy of their single.

The story goes that guitar legend Bert Weedon helped the girls secure the Decca contract. I put this to Bert, and he has absolutely no recollection of it ever happening.

The follow-up 45 was to be "Teenage Dreamer", with a Christmas song entitled "Panda" on the reverse, sadly it never materialised.

"I remember going into the recording studio and the backing band saying they wish they could change places with us. I didn't understand it at the time and it's only now I realise what a great opportunity we had. At the time we were very innocent and very naïve and I don't think we really realised what we were involved in"
Mary McGlynn

24

One Fine Day (Decca)-Shel Naylor
Love Hit Me (Decca)-The Orchids (pic1)
Mirror, Mirror (Decca)-Pinkerton's Colours (pic4)
Take A Heart (Pye)- The Sorrows (pic 5)
So Much In Love (Decca)-The Mighty Avengers
I Remember You (Columbia)-Frank Ifield
Edelweiss (Colombia)-Vince Hill
Heatwave (Polydor)-Bev Jones (pic 6)
Acapulco 1922 (Decca)-Johnny B Great & The Goodmen (pic 3)
Now Is The Time (Phillips)-Martin Cure & The Peeps

Apple Blossom Time (Decca)-The Pickwicks (pic 2)
Rocking Horse (Decca)-Pinkerton's Colours
A Man's Gotta Stand Tall (Colombia)-The Four Matadors
Traitor in Disguise (Decca)- Sue & Mary
The Importance of Your Love (Columbia)-Vince Hill
Lovesick Blues (Columbia)-Frank Ifield
You're Old Enough (Decca)-The Pickwicks (pic 2)
Gonna Make Him Mine (Decca)-The Orchids
House For Sale (Decca)-Lynne Curtis
(Walking Thru) The Sleepy City (Decca)-The Mighty Avengers

The Stormbreakers/ The Establishment
Nuneaton
Formed in 1962 and got to support the likes of Screaming Lord Sutch, The Hollies, The Undertakers, Emily Ford and the Checkmates and the Pretty Things. 1964 they took on former Vampires vocalist Johnny Washington and reinvent themselves as Johnny Washington and The Establishment.

Photos– left the boys in France with some rather unfortunate writing. Below as they were in 2006.

"We had the foresight to get ourselves a good PA system as soon as possible", reveals Keith, "It paid off, one gig in Stoke-On-Trent we were supporting Brian Poole and The Tremeloes and they asked if they could borrow our PA. We had a 100-watt system; theirs was a tiny 50-watt, both pretty puny by today's standards". **Keith Gudger**

When promoter Vince (Martin) Holliday sent the The Stormbreakers to France, they ended up stopping in a Hotel that doubled as a brothel. When Vince sent Birmingham band the Chads to France they ended up stopping in a completely different Hotel that doubled as a brothel.

The Atlantics/ The Werewolves
Coventry
One of the city's first rock' n' roll outfits, based around the energetic vocalist Johnny Martin and guitarist Don Kerr, Mick Calcott-bass, Eddie Milton-rhythm guitar and Tony Chambers-drums. Sorrows guitarist Pip Witcher was later a member. Don and Johnny would eventually leave to join the Reg Calvert venture Freddie Were and the Werewolves.

Photos– below, Johnny and Don in action as the Werewolves, bottom on stage (literally) as the Atlantics, insert Don (left) and John as they look today.

Don came up with the name the Atlantics, giving a British slant to the American trend of naming bands after classic cars; the car in question is the Austin Atlantic A90

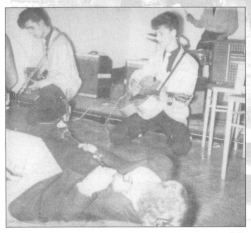

"We had a lot of fun with Reg and the Werewolfes, but we moved on", Said Don, "we did a lot of things music-wise, Johnny got to back Gene Vincent at The Orchid Ballroom and he eventually formed a country band The Big City Boys, as for me well I joined the Brook Brothers and played on the hit singles War Paint and Ain't Gonna Wash for A Week. I joined Stavely Makepeace in the late sixties".
Don Kerr

27

The Peeps
Coventry

By 1965 the Sabres had transformed into The Peeps and were signed to Philips Records by influential bandleader Cyril Stapleton, They released the great 'Freakbeat' single "Now Is The Time", it never charted here for The Peeps, but the influential Australian beat band Ray Brown and the Whispers did a cover of it as the B-side of their Australian number one "In The Midnight Hour". They had morphed into the The Rainbows by 1969.

Photos–Various shots of the Peeps, below that very single.

Jimi Hendrix once supported the Peeps in York University in 1966, though a year later when Hendrix-mania was gripping the UK, the roles were reversed when they supported him in Sweden.

"It was nice with the Peeps, we had our first Record Deal on Phillips, and released five records and appeared on the TV Shows, Thank Your Lucky Stars and Juke Box Jury and did lots of tours of Scandinavia". **Martin Cure**

Tony Martin and his Echo 4
Coventry
Tony Martin and His Echo Four, had been playing the local and national circuits, including a prime show at Coventry Theatre supporting Brian Poole and The Tremeloes. Local impresario Larry Page spotted them, Rod Simpson and Malcolm Watts left and John Miles came onboard and they became the Pickwicks.

Photos– Above Rod, John, Malc and Alan, right, Alan on stage.

A former printer, Tony began his musical career in a skiffle band. Tony Martin and the Echo 4 became the Pickwicks, when they quit he joined the band The Clouds.

In 1988 whilst visiting a relation in Myton Hospice, John Miles saw a face he barely recognised, it was Tony Martin. "We sat and talked about the old days, it was so good to see him again. I went back a few days later with Alan Gee our Rhythm guitarist, we took our guitars along and sang "Apple Blossom Time" with Tony one last time, it was magical but so very sad. A month later Tony was gone, but he will never be forgotten".
John Miles

The Pickwicks
Coventry
Began life as The Tony Martin and His Echo Four, before donning top hats and frock-coats under the management of Larry Page. They released two good freakbeat singles on Decca and one on Warner Brothers. Though it was their B-sides that really hit the mark, with "Hello Lady" (The flip side of You're Old Enough) positively rocks along in a 12 bar boogie style. John Miles lead vocals are spot on dirty and gritty, freakbeat at it's very best.

Photos– Below an original Pickwicks promo picture (Malc, Tony,John & Alan), and re-created in 2005, right, an ultra rare pic of Tony live on stage in the gear.

"We were on stage at this smallish club, doing our usual thing, when suddenly Tony Martin started going wild, he was leaping about with his bass still playing. I was knocked out I though Tony's well into it tonight, this was pre-Hendrix but he was doing all his kind of stuff, going mental. It turned out though that that he had leant against some heating pipes at the back of the stage and burnt the skin off his neck, but like a good trooper he had continued to play"! **John Miles**

Pickwick singles are highly collectable, because all over the Internet it is claimed a certain Jimmy Page played guitar on them. Although a great session man the future Axe-person for Led Zeppelin never played on any Pickwicks record, it was a guy called Harry Friar. So that's just lopped £50 off my copy of "Little By Little".

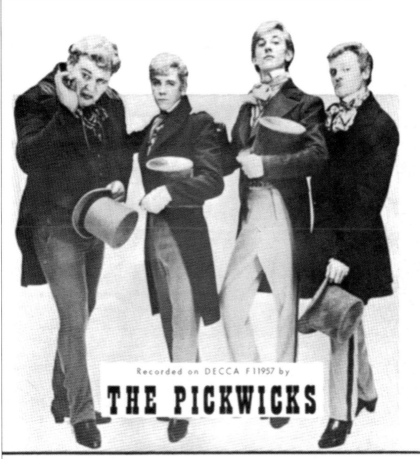

A rare copy of the sheet music to "You're Old Enough", from the Pickwicks.

The Sabres
Coventry

The Sabres consisted of "Q" Martin Cure (vocals), Steve Jones (guitar), Graham Amos (bass) Paul Wilkinson (drums) and former Zodiacs guitarist Terry Wyatt (guitar). Formed in 1960 they were prolific players, even becoming part of a travelling circus. They became The Peeps in 1965.

Photo-below left the Sabres on stage at the Wolfe, below right, at the circus, and bottom a promo handout Steve, Martin, Graham & Paul.

"The Sabres became part of Sir Robert Fossett's Circus in 1962 and toured with it for seven months. We did a 15 minute set to drag in the older kids, and it was during the Jelly Baby craze that Ringo of The Beatles had initiated. So kids would throw tons of Jelly Babies at us. Our set was immediately followed by the elephants, and their keeper hated us because the elephants didn't like walking on the jelly babies and it was hard to get them to perform. It was an interesting seven months, we learnt a lot of things and as we were part of the circus we all had to muck in and help put the tents up. Though I don't think we ever really fitted in, but it was all good press for us". **Martin Cure**

"THE SABRES"

Their Manager Frank Jones (father of their guitarist and main song-writer Steve), was known for creating some fantastic press for the band, much of it unfounded. "He came up with some great press stories", admits Martin Cure," Like the one about us travelling 8,000 miles to tour Eastern Europe and being the second British band to play in Czechoslovakia. None of it was true, but it made great press and got us noticed".

32

The Sorrows
Coventry

The first Coventry band to attain a top 20 hit, with the brooding Take A Heart in 1965. The band consisted of former Hawkes vocalist Don Maughn (Fardon), Pip Witcher lead guitar, Phil Packham former Vampires) bass, plus Bruce Finlay drums and Terry Jukes rhythm guitar. When Fardon left to pursue a solo career, Roger Lomas joined and the band became huge in Italy.

Photos-right, The Sorrows mark I (Don, Phil, Wes, Bruce & Pip), below Mark II, with Roger (front). Bottom, The lads (Phil, Rog, Pip & Wes) in 2005.

Pip's mum gave the band their name when she first heard the practising and called them a sorrowful lot – hence the name "The Sorrows".

"It was fantastic to walk into the local newsagent, where I would buy N.M.E. every week, but this time was different!! I just couldn't wait to turn to the chart page, ran down excitedly and there we were straight in at no 21, how cool was that"? **Wes Price**

Bob Tempest and The Buccaneers.
Coventry

Bob Davidson, Tony Beard, they along with Colin Kingsbear, Louie Woods, Phil Packham and Mal Jenkins formed the band that would become Bob Tempest and The Buccaneers. Tony became a record plugger for Don Arden, and ELO road manager.

Photos– Below The boys on stage, bottom, Tony Beard now a big fund-raiser for Coventry's Myton Hospice.

Former Buccaneer Phil Packham went on to find chart success with The Sorrows and drummer Malc Jenkins joined the Tony Martin and his Echo Four then Decca recording band The Pickwicks.

"They were glorious days" reveals Tony, "at the Orchid we shared the bill with Johnny Kidd, Wee Willie Harris and Oh Boy favourite Cuddly Dudley. Then we got to play further a field and met the likes of Eden Kane, Marty Wilde, Shane Fenton and the Dave Clark Five. I continued to be one of the groups rhythm guitarists, (the band were unique in having a lead guitarist and two rhythm guitarists), but I took on the extra role of manager and got the bookings too". **Tony Beard**

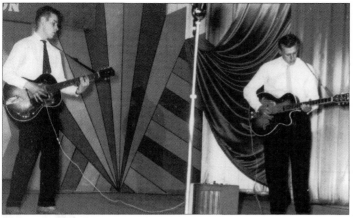

The Vendor Twins
Coventry
After a year of playing together in The Ramblers, Roy and Graham Harrity formed the duo the Vendor Twins in 1962 (they chose 'Vendor' as they were known for playing the song The Peanut Vendor).

Photos-Above the Vendors in action, below Roy in 2006, and that signed photo.

One night we were at the Bamber Club on Foleshill Road, guitar legend Bert Weedon was there setting up and he heard us warming up. He must have liked what he had heard, because he asked us to back him. He lived in Coventry at the time, Allesley way I believe so it was easy for him to go to gigs all around the country. So he told us what he wanted to play and gave us our cues off we went. He was good enough to sign a picture of himself" **Roy Harrity**

BERT WEEDON
TOP RANK RECORDS

Bert Weedon was Britain's guitar pioneer, and his 'Play in a Day' tutorial has inspired millions of budding musicians to pick up the guitar. I contacted him about living in Coventry and he replied, "Yes we did have a second home in Allesley, Nr Coventry for some years".

The Zodiacs
Coventry

One of the, if not the hardest working bands in the area. They have been together for nearly 50 amazing years, and were one of the first few rock 'n' roll bands in the City. Maurice Redhead, and Terry Wyatt have remained core members but many like Steve Jones, Nigel Lomas and Olly Warner have all been Zodiacs at some point. They appeared on New Faces in 1977 singing the Steve Jones and Rod Bainbridge song "Last Night we Called It A Day". Unlike most of the bands in this book, the Zodiacs are still a going concern, how cool is that!

Photos– Below from Small Faces, middle Maurice, Nigel and Terry in 2005, bottom, the boys in 1974

Terry Wyatt and Steve Jones were both original members of The Sabres.

Original drummer Nigel Lomas went on to be a member of The Goodmen, Clouds,The Eggy and Renegade.

"I had a call from a friend Tommy Marshall who worked at The Sound Centre music shop, he had been approached by The Shadows people who were appearing that night at Coventry Theatre. Hank Marvin was looking for a replacement diode bulb for his Morley effects pedal. Tommy knew that I was the only person who always carried spares. When he told me it was for Hank Marvin I thought he was having a laugh? After about the third frantic phonecall I began to believe him. I took the diode to Coventry Theatre, and wandered onto the stage where the Shad's were sound checking. Marvin asked if he could help me, I replied I think I can help you and produced the spare. The band were so grateful they offered me tickets for the show that night". **Terry Wyatt**

"Pinkertons did a total of 4 Top Of The Pops", explains Tom, "I always used to like to go to make-up for a free hair cut shampoo etc. They were really good, but they always did everyone's hair in rollers, even the newscasters. One time they gave me a bouffant style of the day and it stuck right up in the air looking really silly. Julie Rogers the singer, was taking the mickey out of me mercilessly in the canteen. We stayed over after the show on one occasion and watched the 'Stones do an insert for the following week (Paint it Black). I was very impressed with Jagger and very unimpressed with Brian Jones. I remember being surprised how small the audience was". **Tom Long**

Pinkerton's Assorted Colours
Rugby

Originally called the Liberators, Reg Calvert took over as manager and they became the multi-coloured Pinkerton's Assorted Colours, They signed to Decca and released a series of high-quality singles, including the big hit Mirror Mirror (9), the lesser hit Don't Stop Loving Me Baby (50), and the one that should have been number one spot but failed to chart, Magic Rocking Horse. Many of their songs were punctuated with the original sound of an electric autoharp. They changed their name to the Flying Machine in the mid sixties and scored an America number 5 with Smile A Little Smile For Me.

Bass man Stewart Colman, well he went on to be a successful DJ at Radio One. Later moving onto production (his production credits have included, Cliff Richards, Billy Fury, Shakin' Stevens and Kim Wilde). He now works as a producer in Nashville.

Photos– Top left on Top Of The Pops, top right, on Ready Steady Go-right, an historic photo (Barry, Tom & Tony) reunited in 2005, first time in 40 years.

Carol and the Electrons
Coventry
Formed at school as the Electrons in the early sixties. With the addition of girl vocalist Carol Saunders they became Carol and the Electrons. They demoed for Tony Hatch at Pye and played a lot on the Leicester club scene and building a huge fan base there.

Photos– Below with Carol (Brian is second right), bottom right a pre-Carol line-up, below right Barry (left) & Alan now.

"We decided we needed a female singer", reveals Alan Johnson," Barry's dad was a mobile greengrocer and one of his customers was Jack Wilkinson the then entertainment secretary of the Hen Lane Club. There was a young girl called Carol Saunders who sang at the club and Jack recommended her to us and she joined the band and we became Carol and The Electrons. The Hen Lane Club was actually the first place we played in the full line-up, which was around 1963". **Alan Johnson**

Guitarist Brian Whittle who looked extraordinary like Coventry yo-deller Frank Ifield went on to be part of Eyes Of Blues.

Barry now plays bass with "The Legends" the backing band for Lonnie Donegan tribute act Paul Leegan.

Woody Allen And the Challengers
Leamington Spa

Leamington's top beat band, known for their 'twin' guitar sound. For seven months the band were fronted by a young Spanish girl singer named Rosalinda Kasparavicius (pre-dating the 'tiny' Spanish invasion from Los Bravos with Black is Black by three years). They appeared on the TV show For Teenagers Only on two occasions.

Photos– Above the Challengers on stage and with Rosalinda, below, reunited at Call Up The Groups, Coventry, in 2006.

Lynne Curtis of the Mustangs fame was once a temporary member of the Challengers.

"As with many bands of that era we built our act around playing a healthy slab of cover songs from the current hit parade. However we did get into the recording session on three occasions, and recorded That's Love and Lovers Don't Pay (the respective A and B sides to their one and only single), plus No Other Baby, I Beg Of You, Matchbox and April In Portugal".
Bob Saunders

Shel Naylor
Coventry
17 year old Rob Woodward, won a recording deal as a prize at Coventry's Orchid Ballroom. Within weeks, he had Larry Page as manager, had signed to Decca and become Shel Naylor. He released two excellent singles, How Deep is The Ocean and the Dave Davies song One Fine day. Both failed to chart but Rob would eventually form Stavely Makepeace, and later score a number one with his band Lieutenant Pigeon.
Photo's-below right, posing Shel, below right, Rob in 2005, below left Shel in action

When I first saw Rob Woodward (Shel Naylor)" reveals Larry Page, "I thought he was the closest thing I had ever seen to Elvis Presley and so talented. It was very important to me to try and get him off the ground. We had no trouble at all getting public reaction, but nationally and record-wise it certainly wasn't easy in those days". **Larry Page**

One Fine Day is now valued at £100 in mint condition, due mainly to Jimmy Page's session guitar work and the Kinks connection.

ONE FINE DAY

by DAVE DAVIES

Recorded

by

SHEL

NAYLOR

on

DECCA

F11856

2/6

EDWARD KASSNER MUSIC CO. LTD.

SOLE SELLING AGENTS:

KASSNER ASSOCIATED PUBLISHERS LTD. 25, DENMARK ST. LONDON W.C.2.

This is an original, and very rare copy of the sheet music to Shel Naylor's second 1964 single "One Fine Day". Written by Dave Davies of the Kinks fame.

41

Don Fardon
Coventry

Former lead vocalist with the Sorrows. His powerful vocal style saw him not only chart in the UK twice, but also in America with the ultimate native American protest song Indian Reservation. His first UK hit Belfast Boy was a tribute to footballing legend George Best.

Don stands at 6'7" is probably one of the industries tallest singers, even the towering Mick Fleetwood is shorter at just 6'5".

He released Coventry Boy in 2006, an anthology of his career from the Sorrows to the present day and the re-release of Belfast Boy.

Photos-above right, Don as he looks today, above left, Don during his solo days.

.

"I was disillusioned with the business, Don reveals," As I had served an apprenticeship in engineering I got a nine to five job at Whickman's, swapping my Jaguar for a more modest Morris Minor. It eventually ended up falling to pieces in the road". He was eventually coaxed back to the industry signing with top London manager Eve Taylor and secured a record deal with CBS and set about releasing the single "It's been Nice Loving You" a song penned by the great Burt Bacharach (with arrangements by Percy Faith), unfortunately Pye Records claimed that Don was still on their label (a throwback to the Sorrows days). Eventually Pye would back down and the single was released, but despite having the weight of Bacharach & Faith behind it, it failed to do dent the charts.
Don Fardon

Vince Hill
Coventry
A true professional and a real gentleman. Vince began as a member of the Raindrops. Finding fame as a solo artist and TV regular. His hits have included Edelweiss, Roses of Picardy and the Importance of Your Love.

Photos– left Vince in his hey day, and Vince up to date below.

Edelweiss is one of the most popular songs to be played at funerals.

When Edelweiss hit big a battle began with his old record company Pye who released the five year old recording of If You Knew and claimed it was the follow up to Edelweiss!

I was born in Coventry and went to Hen Lane School as it was then, my first tentative notes in front of an audience were in a pub in Margate, of all places. It was aptly called The Prospect. It's just a car park now I understand .My mother cajoled me into entering a Talent Contest which I won the first prize was a week's holiday at the pub the second prize was 2 weeks as they say! Having got the taste for this singing lark I took it quite seriously and had lessons with Ivy Fitton and soon started singing around the local pubs and clubs. Hen Lane Club The Bantam, especially The Bantam, The Unicorn Club and Rowleys Green are still vivid memories for me. I soon started to stretch my wings though Cox Street Club, Radford Club, all round the Midlands and up as far as Sheffield in Yorkshire" **Vince Hill**

Frank Ifield
Coventry
Of all Coventry's musical icons Frank Ifield remains it's most endearing, he remains the city's most successful artist. He had clocked up three consecutive number ones, long before the Beatles had a whiff of the charts. I Remember You, Lovesick Blues and The Wayward Wind will be forever associated with Frank and his amazing yodel.

Photo-Frank and another Cov Kid DJ Brian Matthew.

The distinctive harmonica on I Remember You was an in joke because it's actually the first few bars of Waltzing Matilda! It was played by Harry Pitch, he would later be heard playing on the 1970 Mr Bloe hit Groovin´ with Mr Bloe and on the TV theme to Last of the Summer Wine.

"Throughout my entire career the generous people of Coventry and the Midlands have been my great support and I have played there countless times. Yet one show in particular stands out It was in 1967 when I played the Coventry Theatre. This was the "Birthday Show" which ran from October to November. Significant for several reasons: It was the 30th birthday of the actual Theatre which, I was informed, opened on the very day and date that I was born. Then, during the finale of the opening night on the 6th October, Ted Rogers announced to me that my son Mark was born. To cap it off our closing night on November 30 was also a celebration of my own 30th birthday. Today, although I live back in Australia, my mind is filled with the many fond memories of my life in England and the close friendships I have made and I make it my business to return as often as possible. A fellow Coventarian" **Frank Ifield**

The Vampires
Coventry

Actually began operation in the 1950's, and in doing so became one of the first rock n roll combo's in the area.

Photos-left–Geoff Baker, Phil Packham, Barry Bernard and Vince Martin. Insert, the Vamps. Below the Vampires circa 2005

"We got a lot of attention, as we were the only rock 'n' roll band about. It was like a magnet, the kids were buying the records of the day, but rarely got a chance to see any live bands. So that's were we came in, of course we had problems at first, it seems strange now but this was all new then and some people considered rock 'n' roll the devils music. Some places wouldn't even have us on".
Vince Martin, The Vampires

Despite never releasing a record, former members of the Vampires had four UK chart hits between them (1 for Barry Bernard with Pinkertons Colours 2 for Barry with Jigsaw and one for Phil Packham with the Sorrows).

When the late great John Peel died, he left a box of 142 - 7" vinyl singles, believed to be his favourites, amongst them was the single So Much In love. When you look at the company it was keeping, (I refer to the likes of Elmore James, MC5, the Beatles and of course The Undertones), it's easy to see what an impressive legacy the band left behind them.

I asked the legendary and very elusive Andrew Loog Oldham, if he remembered the Mighty Avengers?, he replied, "Of course, often and fondly". I asked him if he felt they could have been bigger than they actually were? He replied in his usual delphian way," We had good songs, and as I recall , had a nice time getting them done, and you can still hear it, it doesn't get much better than that".
Andrew Loog Oldham

The Mighty Avengers
Rugby

Rugby's Mighty Avengers, became the first local band to hit the charts in 1964, with the Jagger/Richards composition "So Much In Love". Despite their strong connections with the Stones and Andrew Loog Oldham , they were never to chart again (until they morphed into Jigsaw that is).

Main Photo-Biffo Beech, Tony Campbell, Kevin Mahon & Mike Linnell. Insert photos-Biffo, Tony and Kevin 2005/2007

All hail to the Coventry Sound, circa 1964, what a night that must have been. The word is that the Orchids never played.

47

Dusty Springfield was once in Beverley's dressing room and was told to leave because It belonged to Miss Jones. Beverley tells the story," I had turned up at the television studio to appear on Disc A Go Go pop show and Dusty Springfield was in my dressing room. I was told she would be asked to leave but I said tell her to take her time, When I got into my dressing room there was a message across the mirror in red lipstick saying Best wishes Beverly, Love Dusty S x".

Bev Jones
Coventry
Bev got to release a stack of great singles in the early 60's, including "Heatwave", and "Wait Till My Bobby Gets Home". She was (and indeed still is) the owner of a superbly powerful voice.Photos-above with The Goodmen, Don Kerr, Nigel Lomas and Olly Warner. Insert Bev in 2005.

"We all could see Jeff was a bit tasty as a guitarist, he used to play "Baby Please Don't Go" and he totally nailed it, he was spot on. He was very shy and naive in those days, and he refused to sing, we did tease him a lot. I think that 18 months with The Chads gave him a good grounding, we kept in touch for a long time, though sadly he never seems keen to acknowledge his roots as a member of the Chads".
Noddy

The bands manager was none other than former Vampires front-man Vince Martin.

The Chads
Birmingham
They formed from the Sundowners in the late 1950's in Birmingham, and proceeded to play a ton of live dates in the Coventry area. They were looked after by Reg Calvert for a short while, suitably attired as The Merry Men backing Robby Hood (Mike West). In 1965 Mick Adkins finally settled down to married life and he was replaced by a fresh-faced guitarist called Jeff Lynne. Mick passed away in 2007, god bless.

Top and bottom photo-the Chads in France 1964, and above right reunion time in Coventry 2005.

Ray King
Coventry
Coventry's very own 'Soul Man', who was a prime mover in the creation of The Specials and the Selecter. His band the Ray King Soul Band. Played the likes of the Playboy Club. Releasing a live album recorded at the venue. He remains with his finger on the musical pulse of Coventry.

Photos-Ray in the 60's (right) and present day (left).

The Ray King Soul Band once pulled a bigger crowd at Coventry's Locarno than even the Rolling Stones.

It was quite normal for Ray and his band to play three gigs a night, like The Walsgrave Hotel, the Craven and the Matrix were three that sprung to mind.

"We knew we had something going on", reveals Ray, "We were so tight in our playing, I was able to control the band with just a slight hand movement, and their eyes were on me all the time. David Owen became our manager and we played the Lanch Polytechnic (now Coventry University) and they always asked us back. We supported people like Georgie Fame and later Julie Driscoll/Brian Auger & The Trinity". The bands reputation grew to the point when they were asked by the famous Playboy Club in London to perform. "David our manager told us to take some time off to rehearse for the gigs", reveals Ray, "we were booked to play Thursday, Friday, Saturday and Sunday nights. So instead of repeating the sets I decided to rehearse four forty-five minute shows, and perform a different one every night". **Ray King**

SEVENTIES

LOCARNO COVENTRY DEC 2 1971

Peppermint Kreem
Coventry

The Albrigton brothers Arthur (Modie) and his brother Roye Both are now located in Germany, but their roots are firmly entrenched in Coventry and it's music scene. Modie a top class guitarist and blues harp player began with the local band Makeshift. Before moving onto Peppermint Kreem a 5 piece rock band that headlined a Memorial Park concert in the mid sixties. They even recorded their own rock opera Revelations 2001 (at Time Machine Studios Earlsdon). Members included founder Paul Kennelly, Tom Ryan, Dave Fairclough and Ray Haywood. Modie went on to join the likes of Nuts and Bolts, Crossfire and Heaven Sent a club band that would include Rodney Byers in its ranks. Roye joined German based prog rockers Nektar.

Photos– Below right Peppermint Kreem, below left Modie all revved up and ready to play, bottom, a more laid-back Modie in 2005.

"I met Paul Kennelly and we started playing together Bands like Plague Makeshift Peppermint Kreem I then played for New City Sounds and others After this I went to Germany in 1976 I am also well known in Germany the part were I live".
Modie Albrighton

I remember going to the Coventry theatre when I was 8 years old to see a pantomime called Jack and the Beanstalk playing was Larry Adler he threw small harmonics out and said anyone that has one come on the stage when I got on the stage with him I told him I had my own so I did a duet with him my GOD I wish there was a chance to make a recording but that was not possible in these times.

Lieutenant Pigeon
Coventry
With Mouldy Old Dough, Lieutenant Pigeon had created a perfect novelty song but with the addition of Rob's Mother in the band the concept had been extended and sound and image merged together perfectly to create a novelty classic that would see the band top the charts for four weeks.

Photos– bottom left, Nige and Rob 2005, both the others are from 1972.

"We were grateful for the Mouldy Old Dough hit ", reveals Rob Woodward. "With Decca on our side at this time I felt we could muster a lower half of the top twenty. When it hit the number one spot I was knocked sideways -to say the least! I must say that reality did kick in though having to follow up a number one hit. It definitely had the cards stacked against it -as far as the UK was concerned, this of course proved to be the case with Desperate Dan reaching only number 17, the classic double-edged sword"! **Rob Woodward**

When Mouldy Old Dough hit the top spot in the UK, Chuck Berry was doing the same in the US charts with My Ding A-ling. That meant that both singles on either side of the Atlantic had been recorded in Coventry, Mouldy Old Dough in Kingsway, Stoke and My Ding A-ling at The Locarno in Coventry City Centre.

53

The Rainbows
Coventry

When Coventry Beat band The Peeps knew it was the time for change they reinvented themselves as a progressive band in the mould of Traffic called The Rainbows. With sculptured hair, bizarre eye make-up and multi-coloured flowing robes they moved their base to London. They just about scraped into the 70's, before becoming Still life.

Photos– Above The Rainbows on stage, below left a promo shot.

"We released a lot of stuff on CBS Records. We wore silly clothes and make-up for photo Sessions, and as I recall we spent a lot of time in Germany at the "Star Club " in Hamburg in particular. We had lots of great nights with visiting English Bands, like the time Ozzy Osbourne (pre-Sabbath) joined us on stage for a wild finale!! **Martin Cure**

Below Martin joined on stage with Ozzy.

Name Dropping (EMI)-The Flys (pic1)
Sky High (Splash)-Jigsaw (pic 2)
Smokey Mountain Rhythm Revue (Concord)-Stavely Makepeace
Smile a Little smile For Me (Pye)-The Flying Machine
Alright Baby (Magnet)-Stevenson's Rocket
NCB Man (Bell)-A Band Called George
Read About Seymour (Rough Trade)-Swell Maps (pic 3)
Machine (Decca)-Ning
Lovin' and Forgiving (Parlophone)-The Renegades
Rockabilly Hotpot (Decca)-Lieutenant Pigeon

Sun Clog Dance (RCA)-Dando Shaft
Cajun Band (Deram)-Stavely Makepeace
New Day Dawning (CBS)-The Rainbows
Love on the Rebound (Polydor)-The Dodgers
Everybody Knows (Psycho)-The Incredible Kidda Band (pic 4)
Mouldy Old Dough (Decca)-Lieutenant Pigeon
Gangsters (2-Tone)-The Special AKA Vs the Selecter (pic 5)
The Taker (Avatar)-Chevy
Millionaire (Squad)-Squad (pic 6)
You're Still Mine (Spark)-The Eggy

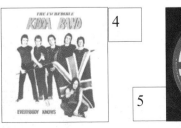

Fresh Maggots
Nuneaton

Despite their name, this duo produced some fine melodic folk/rock. They produced one great album for RCA in 1971. It's now super rare and worth around £400 in mint condition.

Photos– two promotional shots of the Maggots, Leigh on left in both.

"In the winter of 1971 we released our only single Car Song", reveals Leigh. it was a clapping sing-a-long type thing, the music paper Disc seemed to like it, then our manager Mike got bored with us and moved on, we tried to do it on our own but it was difficult especially with full time jobs and by 1972 we just fizzled out". **Leigh Dolphin**

The Song Who's to Die was inspired by a near fatal car accident in Coventry's Eagle Street, and the title of the song Rosemary Hill was inspired by the Kenilworth road of the same name.

A poster from 1971, showing the Fresh Maggots supporting Ra-Ho-Tep (they included the legendary Tim James and Joe Craner in their ranks).

Stevenson's Rocket
Coventry
Began life as a club band, until Pete Waterman took them on and turned them into Coventry's answer to the Bay City Rollers. They scored a top forty with Alright Baby in 1975, so becoming the 'Hitmans' first hit!

Photos– above left, an early line-up of the band, right the 1975 version.

"Monday nights at Tiffanys were a complete eye opener, an amazing time, but we were really green in those days. Teenage girls were throwing bracelets, rings and scarves on the stage at us, I was desperate to give all this stuff back to their rightful owners, until Pete Waterman explained they were gifts from adoring fans and should not be returned!" **Alan Twigg**

Dave Reid reveals that he had a lot of time for Pete Waterman, "because he had a lot of time for us, he was with us for nearly three years solid promoting us on tour. We couldn't ask for more, he often referred to himself as the "sixth rocket". **Dave Reid**

The band once shared an agency in Wolverhampton with Led Zeppelin's rock god Robert Plant, one day a rather bemused Plant walked unmolested through a throng of screaming Stevenson's Rocket fans oblivious to the fact they had just ignored a 25% of the greatest rock band in the world.

Alright Baby faired better on the Radio Luxembourg RTL chart reaching a creditable number 22!

Chevy
Coventry/Leamington
Thus far, the areas most successful heavy rock band. Forever living under the banner of the New Wave Of British Heavy Metal (or N.W.O.B.H.M). They wooed the rock fans and pulled off support slots to Space rockers Hawkwind playing at Cov's Tiffanys in 1980.

Photos-below left Chevy promo picture and below right on stage.

Martin Cure's musical CV looks like a veritable who's who of local bands. From The Sabres, The Peeps, Rainbows, Still Life to Cupids Inspiration.

They gained a prize spot on the EMI Metal For Muthas Vol 2 album with the track Chevy.

"Chevy really came out of Cupids Inspiration. After years of playing covers we decided we wanted to write our own music, so Chevy were formed, with the addition of local guitarist Steve Walwyn (now Dr Feelgood). We released an album called "The Taker" and two singles from the Album. We recorded Two "In Concerts" for the BBC and toured constantly in the UK. Excellent band, played some fantastic gigs but with naff Management it was bound to end in tears.Folks. Chas the drummer left and we replaced him with Ted Duggan. That's Rock & Roll and we carried onwith Chevy MkII for a while, but eventually ran out of steam and > turned into Red on Red". **Martin Cure**

Pete Waterman
Coventry
Along with Two Tone, Pete is Coventry's top music icon. You name it he's done it, from Djing at the Locarno to becoming one of the worlds most successful producers. Discovering Kylie, and collecting trains, there is no stopping the Water Man.

Photos– bottom, Pete during his 14-18 period, below a more up-to-date Pete.

Pete's first ever success story chart-wiser was with Coventry teeny bop band Stevenson's Rocket. The song was Alright Baby. This was when Pete was at Magnet records.

He was the first to discovered The Specials in Coventry and promoted them, to an unready world, they would have to wait a while before they hit big.

In 2005, I contacted many Coventry musicians in the view of launching a Coventry Music Exhibition in the City. Meetings have now started to make this a reality. Here is the great message of support from Dr. Pete Waterman OBE himself.

"I wholeheartedly endorse the concept of having a room in the Herbert Art Gallery & Museum dedicated to local music. I think that it is vital to protect and preserve our heritage in order for it to be presented accurately to future generations.

Pete Chambers is a great ambassador for Coventry and has the interests of the city at the heart of this campaign - he deserves to succeed and I wish him well."

Indian Summer
Coventry
Our own prog' rock band, released one great album for RCA's Neon label, at one point the band included Wez Price formerly of the Sorrows.

Photos– top left   Bob Jackson, top right Malcolm Harker and Paul Hooper, below left Colin Williams, below right Indian Summer mark II, insert Wez Price.

At The Carnon Downs Festival in Truro on 21st August 1971. Indian Summer were sixth on the bill and an unheard of band called Queen were eighth !

"Recording the album at Trident studios was a thrill but because it was really our first time doing a proper professional recording we probably let a lot of stuff pass which we should have taken more time over. I remember the "Time is Money" ethic being banded about by record company people, so we were under some pressure to get it done as soon as possible. I recall that we were recording at all times of the day and well into the night on some occasions". **Paul Hooper**

Squad

Coventry

Cov's number one punk band, famous for including Special-to-be Terry Hall in it's line-up, though his replacement Gus Chambers would become the mainstay of the band. They released two great singles (Millionaire and Red Alert) in the seventies, and appeared on the Sent From Coventry LP singing Flasher. Gus went on to form 21 Guns, much later joining metal giants Grip Inc.

Photos– below, Danny, Gus & Rob on stage, insert Mr George's ticket and bottom a young pre-punk look.

Whilst Grip Inc were resting Gus formed the band "Squad 21" the name of course is made up from former bands Squad and 21 Guns, they released one album entitled Skullduggery. It includes reworkings of 21 Guns, The Flasher and Millionaire.

"We were sitting in this club with a couple of band members, when in burst a guy with a huge kitchen knife screaming all punks must die because they had killed Elvis Presley. No one was hurt but it shows what a negative role the media played in it's portrayal of punks". "There were however some positives in that time" Gus says. "The race barriers was smashed down during this period and there was nothing stronger than a united front". **Gus Chambers**

MR. GEORGE NITE SPOT

SUPER NEW WAVE – PUNK SPECIAL

WITH

SQUAD

FREE ADM. BEFORE 10·30 20p AFTER

MIN. AGE 18   LIC 8pm – 2am

"I joined a new band (this time switching to bass) Fagin Quill (all these crazy names were my doing!), an explosive 3 piece, playing blues/rock performing self-penned songs and with our own lightshow (run by Maurice Murphy). We ran a club in our native Rugby but played as far away as London in blues clubs and universities and many times in Coventry where we were once described in an ad: "...don't miss this fantastic group with a lightshow to end all lightshows..." and that was following the incredible Jigsaw!! **Andy Hayward**

When Andy got a job in London he used to commute, and often talked to Pete Waterman on the train journey.

Fagin Quill
Rugby
Rugby musician Andy Hayward had been rockin' in various bands since 1963. Like Sam Spade, The Tea Set and finally this three piece Fagin Quill. They were Psychedelic and proud of it.

Photos– Below live on stage (Andy far right), insert business card, left the ever popular posed promo shot.

Renegade
Coventry
Included the Lomas brothers (Roger & Nigel) and Pip Witcher and Mick East-bury. Never really set out to be a glam rock band, but certainly looked like it. They released one single in this set-up, although the Lomas's had used the name for a previous single Loving & Forgiving.

Photos– below left a montage of live shots of the band (top- Rog and Pip, bot-tom-Mick and Nigel) Below right, the band in a leather posing moment.

Bizarrely the 'flip' side of A Little Rock n Roll, entitled My Revolution, found its way onto the glam rock compilation album-Glitter From The Litter Bin.

Roger made all the bands leather clothes himself, all by hand!

"We were signed to George Martin's production company called Air Lon-don, who had their studios in Oxford Street, London. We had just one sin-gle called "A Little Rock 'N' Roll" on the Dawn Label in 1974. We didn't intentionally set out to be classed as a Glam-Rock band, but after looking at the photos, you'd have to be blind not to see that we obviously looked like one. It was just the fashion of the time & most rock bands looked like a bit like that really". **Roger Lomas**

Dando Shaft
Coventry
No one ever performed folk music like this before. Dando managed to create a 'heavy prog' vibe using just acoustic instruments. The band was made up of very competent musicians and the superb vocals of Leamington's Polly Bolton. They released a handful of original and exciting albums.

Photos-Top left Dando , with Kevin in the foreground, to right Kevin as he is to-day and below, an intimate live show.

The name Dando Shaft is a character from a bawdy American paperback.

Coventry guitar-maker Bob Armstrong makes Kevin's guitars.

Dando Shaft albums are hugely collectable, with some worth up to £200!

"John Martyn was just fantastic, he really liked us and helped Dando Shaft in those early days, his promoter Sandy Glennon was also a pivotal factor in our develop-ment. Sandy got us some studio time at the famous Pye Studios Marble Arch. As luck would have it producer Miki Dallon was there and asked us that marvellous question do you want to make an album? Of course we did", we replied. **Kevin Dempsey**

Rob Armstrong
Coventry
Although Rob is very much a musician, it's for crafting superb guitars he is now best known for. With a client list that includes the late George Harrison, Alvin Lee, Joe Brown, Bert Jansch and Gordon Giltrap, his instruments are much in demand. Each instrument takes from two to three weeks to make, using wood that is at least 25 years old. He uses no power tools, preferring to make each one totally by hand, so no two are alike. He reckons he's made well over 700 instruments to date

Photos– below left, just a couple of examples of Rob's work, below right Rob and his miniature guitar as favoured by George Harrison.

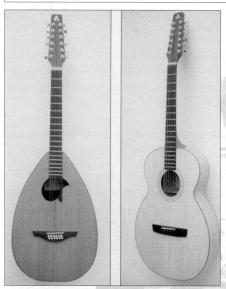

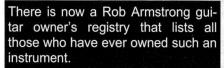

There is now a Rob Armstrong guitar owner's registry that lists all those who have ever owned such an instrument.

"Since I made my first guitar in 1971, I have continued with the same philosophy of making one instrument at a time using basic hand tools. This has given me the freedom to create many variations of stringed instruments. Some simple and functional, some more ornate and complicated. The result is that few instruments are repeated and none duplicated. The possibility of some new insight or understanding of my craft remains my main motivation". **Rob Armstrong**

Despite releasing some 13 singles (on almost as many record labels), "The Scrap Iron Rhythm Revue" CD is their only ever official album.

Their track, Slippery Rock 70's, was used in the soundtrack of the cult film Hot Fuzz.

Stavely Makepeace
Coventry
Nigel Fletcher and Rob Woodward experimented with sound, and produced an exciting series of singles. The basis of this band became the novelty offshoot band Lieutenant Pigeon.

Photos-Above Stavely with Rob (left) and Nigel in cravats, below at the Cathedral, Steve Johnson, Rob, Don, Nigel and Steve Tayton .

"We kept Stavely Makepeace alive as a recording unit during those Lieutenant Pigeon years but now we felt it was time to resume where we'd left off. For a further 5 years we soldiered on but Stavely Makepeace never became the huge success we'd all dreamed about. At the end of 1983, after a total of 13 singles and as many heartbreaks, we finally wound the band down. We remained based in Coventry throughout. It's a great city and ideally placed to reach all the other major cities in the country. At the time of writing, only three of us remain here. That's Don Ker, Rob and myself, but we might soon have to drag Steve Johnson back from Blackburn and Steve Tayton back from France. This is because RPM Records have released 22 of the best of our tracks on a compilation CD The Scrap Iron Rhythm Revue. Stavely Makepeace lives on"! **Nigel Fletcher**

Jigsaw
Rugby
Built around the remains of The Mighty Avengers, the band had a reputation of being a great live act with more than a hint of comedy about them. It would take nearly ten years before they were to hit big with Sky High, a song that charted globally for them, including a number 3 in America.

Photos– Below a promo handout, bottom the guys arrive in Japan, Des, Barry, Clive and Tony.

The name Jigsaw was chosen because "The Mighty Avengers used to play at the Jigsaw club in Manchester when part of the Kennedy Street scene, and I had always thought it would make a good name for a band", reveals Tony

"Clive Scott had approached the Avengers with his song writing abilities, but we realised he was a good keyboard man and sang as well. I only needed a bass player to get operational. I spent three weeks trying to find Barrie Bernard. I had known him well for a number of years and we had talked about working together one day. I eventually found him at the Nags Head in Nuneaton. His first words to me that night were "Tone, I need a job". My reply was "You've got one".
Tony Campbell

The Flys
Coventry
Labelled as punk, but new wave really fitted them much better. They produced a handful of excellent singles and two great albums in the 70's, sadly they never achieved the success they deserved and split in 1980.

Photos– above left, rare promo photo, above right a less rare Flys promo pic, bottom right an up to date Neil O'Connor.

"I received a phone call to ask us if "The Flys" would be interested to open for The Buzzcocks that very same evening at "Mr George". We accepted and with trepidation, we crashed the first chord of our first song in the set and we went down a storm, not one glass crashed around our heads, yeah some gob but, if it can be said, friendly gob. We played the same songs that we'd been playing since a few months, nothing had really changed except, perhaps, we had now become acceptable because of our association, for that night, opening for these new stars of the scene, "The Buzzcocks". They were great. We had such a good time together and after that evening we opened for them for the rest of their tour, EMI saw us and we had our first record contract". **Neil O'Connor**

Former Eurythmic Annie Lennox decided to cover the Lover Speaks song No More I love You's on her 1995 Medusa album. Eventually releasing the song as a single, it achieving a number 2 in The UK and number 23 in The US.

Neil is the brother of Hazel O'Connor, it was he who inspired her to write songs.

In 1995 David The Duetch won the top Entertainer in Coventry award.

The Carltons
Coventry
One of the funniest acts on the local club circuit. The Carlton's came together in 1970, with former Pickwicks guitarist and vocalist Johnny Miles (John the Bomb), Vocalist David Davies (Duetch), Drummer Stan Robinson (Stan the Ram) and Keyboardist Mick McClure (Mick the Dick).

Photos– Top left it's a drag for The Duetch, top right promo shot (from back,Stan, Mick, John and Dave). Insert, The lads in 2005, John, Stan and Dave.

The Carlton's gave their audience's something different. like Stan's deaf ventriloquist act. "I am actually a bit deaf", admits Stan," I had monkey's and all sorts, of course I could never really do it I just put my hand over my mouth when the puppet was supposedly speaking, it always got a huge laugh. The kids loved it. Dressing up in crazy costumes was the order of the day for The Carltons and it often ended up with Duetch dressed as a woman or something similar. **Stan Robinson**

The Innovations
Coventry
The line up looked like this; Graham (the Rat) Rollason Bass and vocals, John Settle lead guitar, Pete Wilson vocals, Alan Wright guitar and Paul Kent on drums. In 1976 they won a talent contest at the Trocadero Night Club at Weston Hall, Bulkington. The personnel changed in 1981 and they became the new Innovations, and included comedy in their act.

Photos– below left, The Innovations, Alan Wright, John Settle, Pete Wilson, Paul Kent & Graham Rollason. Below the Rat right up to date. Bottom The New Innovations.

The New Innovations set about injecting comedy into their act. The introduction of a Laurel and Hardy pastiche (using a screen and a strobe light) was a great success, and became the talk of the town "The first time we did it, recalls Graham, " was at a RAF base, we toyed with the idea of leaving it out and concentrating on just the music. In the end we did it and it went down a storm, they lapped it up. We went on to do it in all the clubs. I've met people that still remember it to this day, it was obviously memorable" **Graham Rollason**

Graham has also played with the bands; Carolina, Joe Beale Blues Band and the Bluesrats. He is a huge Lerry Lee Lewis fan, and has met him many times.

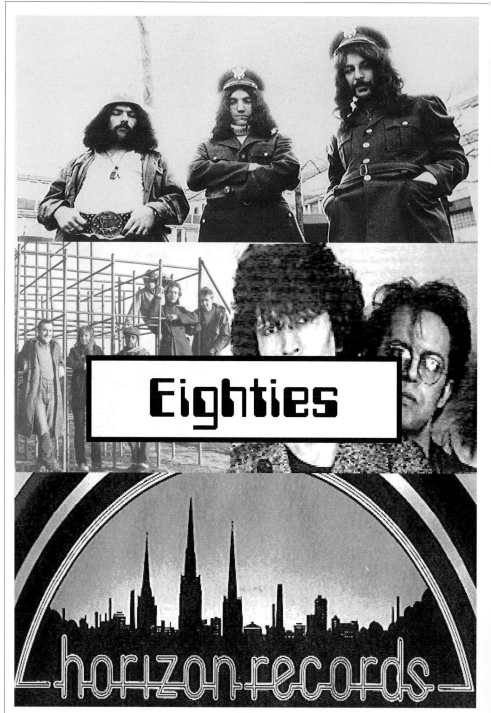

Eighties

horizon records

Apollo Theatre, Coventry

Phil McIntyre by arrangement with
Fair Warning present—
THE STEPS IN TIME TOUR

KING plus Support

Saturday, 6th April 1985 at 7.30

CIRCLE

£4.50

D   36

No Tickets Exchanged nor Money Refunded
No Cameras or Recording Equipment
Official Programmes sold only in the Theatre

Retain this portion

Paul King always dedicated the song (and eventual single) Torture to Barbara Dixon and Elaine Page who would hold the top spot that January effectively robbing King of a number one hit.

King
Coventry
When the Two Tone of the Specials faded, up popped King and their multi-toned Doc Marten boots. King hit the spot, and impressed with their 80's style, clever lyrics and anthemic songs.

Photos– Top left, a rare candid John Hewitt pic from 1983, King ticket, above Paul king at Highfield Rd, right King promo shot.

"King came into official being around 1982" reveals Paul King, "playing the General Wolfe, Dog & Trumpet, the Hope & Anchor & the Belgrade studio theatre as we crafted our sound & style. Locally the one Coventry show that will always top my list had to be the bands Apollo gig in March 1985. The first rock show I had ever been to was David Bowie's performance at the theatre in 1973 in full Ziggy mode. Without wishing to sound clichéd it really did 'change my life' and so Kings show at the height of our chart activity was a full circle in life terms and one I will always remember with affection". **Paul King**

73

Calvary
Coventry

The group was built around Coventry's Mr. Entertainment, Irish born Bob Brolly MBE. Calvary built up an enviable reputation on the club scene, playing locally, nationally and even internationally. Bob currently presents on BBC Coventry & Warwickshire radio and continues to entertain as a solo performer with a strong Irish slant. He's also well known for his fund raising, making literally millions for charity.

Photos– Top and bottom Calvary promotion Hairspray & make-up shots, below Bob in 2007 at the Beeb.

In October 2001 Bob was named Coventry's Citizen Of The Month In November of the same year, Bob was presented with a special Papal Certificate together with a special blessing from the Pope. Both were in recognition of Bob's devoted services to charity.

"Without blowing my own trumpet, we had a great band of musicians. We had Neil from Drops Of Brandy and Ted Duggan on drums, I was surrounded by fantastic musicians over the years. They all made my job of standing at the front very easy". They became the Bass promotion band packing Working Men's clubs every night, as a covers band they had the knack of often performing the songs better live than the original musicians could do. "I was literally working every night of the week, we did a couple of our own gigs, then any night we didn't have a gig Bass took us, So we opened pubs and clubs the length and breath of the country." **Bob Brolly**

Urge
Coventry
A huge favourite on the scene in the 80's, one of the most inventive and original. Included Kevin Harrison, Lynda Harrison. John Westacott and Dave Wankling. Released the highly collectable Revolving Boy. They later signed for Arista Records, Kevin continues to produce high quality music.

Photos-below live at the General Wolfe, Coventry, below in Cologne Germany.

"I remember. Rehearsing at The Binley Oak, Playing regularly at The Wolfe and Lanchester Polytechnic. Hearing 'Revolving Boy' on John Peel on a car radio. Playing in Germany / Barcelona with The Specials & U2 at The Moonlight. Julian Lennon & Zak Starkey coming to see 'urge' at Dingwalls". **Kevin Harrison**

Urge appeared on the Sent From Coventry album with the track Nuclear Terrorist.

Their second single Bobby, was used as a radio theme tune by former City player and manager Bobby Gould.

75

20 Days
Coventry

A trio consisting of Simon O'Grady (vocals & bass) Peter Burke (drums) and John O'Sullivan (vocals & guitar). Had a brand of high-energy guitar based 60's retro rock, and released a four track 12inch EP in 1985 on Cabin's Sonar Label. In 1989 they morphed into 'superband' The Hungry i .

Photos– top, pic by yours truly, probably the best promo pic I ever took. Bottom, Simon, John & Peter.

"We signed with Cabin's in-house label Sonar Records", John reveals, "and released our first record, a 12" E.P. in 1985 with the song "Freefall" as the lead track. Then we secured a residency at the city's Rose & Crown pub. That helped elevate the band's reputation as one of the best live acts in Coventry. One of our 'fans', Horace Panter of the Specials, was nice enough to finance the recording of their entire set at Cabin studios. However, fame and fortune still eluded us. The mid 80s weren't the best time to be a three-piece 60s guitar band, the pop world being dominated at that time by keyboards, big hair and heavy handed synthetic drum sounds! Rather than change our style to please record companies, we chose to please ourselves and remain true to our roots (and starved to death!)" **John O'Sullivan**

Hungry i were included in an REM biography for their unconventional cover version of an unreleased REM song.

76

The Specials
Coventry
The seven piece ska band that really put Coventry on the musical map. More than just a band a whole movement called Two Tone that even gave the City an iconic record label of the same name. They hit the top spot twice with Too Much Too Young and later Ghost Town. Despite a messy break-up they left a legacy that continues to resonate world-wide.

Photos– all taken by the author, top left Lynval and Jerry on stage at the Lanch (now Cov Uni), top right, Nev and Terry about to entrance the same gig, bottom enjoying themselves (at least on stage) at The Butts, Rock Against Racism gig 1981.

Despite their huge success, the Specials never hit the top spot with an album . The first Cov artists to achieve this was The Enemy in July 2007.

" Mr George, The best gig, the best crowd, the best beer.. oh wait, the best beer was at the Domino. Mr Georges, not all the girls were slag's but the beer did taste like.....".**Lynval Golding**

In 2005 Jerry Dammers was kind enough to grant me an interview for my Coventry Telegraph Backbeat column. Apart from a handful of websites, it has never been available elsewhere. As it's still pretty current I have used it here in it's entirety. **Pete Chambers**

Photos-are Jerry in 2006 receiving his Honorary Degree from Coventry University. Left the author with Jerry and Lynval

1.At what age were you when you moved from India to Britain, do you have any strong memories of growing up in Coventry?

I left India aged 2, then lived in Sheffield and came to Coventry aged ten (1965). Obviously I've got loads of memories. I don't know, for some reason I can remember thinking the top floor of multi storey car parks was a good place to hang out when you're a bored teenager.

2.How was your musical background formulated, were your parents an influence at all?

Not that much I don't think, although I'm grateful they sent me for piano lessons. I was rubbish and hated practising, the only thing that interested me was teaching myself blues. It was The Who, The Small Faces, The Kinks, which made me want to be in a band, and I loved soul music, Otis Redding, Sam and Dave, Tamla Motown.

3.How was your interest in reggae, punk and ska nurtured, did it always feel natural to meld punk and ska together or was it a conscious effort ?

I got into reggae from when I first heard it around 1969, Desmond Decker and all that, I was trying to get my school rock band to play it as early as 1971, but no one took reggae seriously in rock circles in those days. Yes it was a conscious effort to combine ska with punk, but it still seemed natural to me. We injected a bit of that funky African offbeat energy, which most rock could do with I reckon.

4.The Specials break up was of course a messy affair, you are often quoted as saying you were just pleased that they stayed together long enough to record Ghost Town. Was there a lot of disappointment on your part, did you feel the Specials suffered a premature death, or was it a relief to work with a new set of musicians?

Some people seem to have forgotten that strictly speaking The Specials didn't actually break up, some of the band left and said I could carry on the name, which is what happened. I suppose at first maybe it seemed like a bit of a relief, because a couple of the band had become impossible to work with by the end, but deep down it was very disappointing. When the Fun Boy Three went "pop" and left the Specials I don't think they really understood the unique position they were in. What they did quite possibly reduced the chances of protest music getting into the pop charts right up to the present day. I also don't think they realise what I was put through trying to keep alive that standard of music, combined with the political ideals, which the Specials had come to represent. I got more than enough grief from a couple of the original Specials for my song-writing and arranging, that resentment was even more crazy from a couple of the replacement members. It was probably a mistake to expect another good live band to come mainly from Coventry, so soon after The Specials and Selecter. We still managed to achieve "The Boiler", the "In the Studio" album, and "Free Nelson Mandela" though, but it took forever and all turned into a bit beyond a nightmare. By the end I was in so much debt to the record company I had to stop recording. I got involved in organising Artists Against Apartheid, which led to the Mandela concerts at Wembley Stadium, so some good did come out of it all in the end. Maybe Terry Hall wouldn't have been as convincing as Stan Campbell singing "Free Nelson Mandela" anyway.

5.Your understandable stance to keep 2 Tone and the Specials as things of the past has often been misconstrued as your disregard towards them. I was personally gratified to hear you tell me that wasn't the case, and that all you have created did indeed give you a great sense of pride. Is this why your remain so protective of the 2 Tone and Specials banners?
I've never had any stance to keep 2 Tone or The Specials as things of the past. The Fun Boy Three took that stance when they left the band. If I'd had my way The Specials might still be making music today, who knows. I'm very proud of the music we made and I still want as many people as possible to hear the proper Specials' records. Anyone who really valued the band would be bound to have a little bit of disregard towards the people who demolished it wouldn't they? Terry Hall now says they didn't really have a reason for leaving. A couple of them went on to rubbish The Specials or me in interviews, then a couple claimed to have formed The Specials (when everyone knows it was me), then a

couple claimed to still be The Specials even though they'd left years earlier. As I understood it they stopped being The Specials when they announced they'd left the band. For them to use the name like they did wasn't fair on the public. They didn't even phone me to see if I might be interested. It was hard to see the thing I'd worked towards for years being pulled back down almost to the level of a pub band. I think it's them that disregarded The Specials, I never did.

6.The talk of a Specials reunion featured heavily in our local press last year, just how frustrating is it to be at the centre of such huge speculation?

If many people had actually heard those later records made under The Specials' name they'd be able to work out how much I contributed to the real Specials, and what a massive effort it would take, from everyone, to get it back to anything which could really be taken seriously again. There's a web site which was set up at the time they were doing the rounds as the Specials and I think the guy who set it up was given a bit of a false impression. I don't know if there's really been that much speculation, it's hard to say how many of the public are really losing sleep over it. I wish, as much as anyone, that we were all young and The Specials were still together, just like the good old days at the start; but the practical reality is it's quite late in the day. People have got new careers, some have moved on musically, some have hardly played for years, there are health problems, some voices may be damaged, some people's memory never was that good, and we don't even live on the same continent. A lot of fans who loved the Specials don't want to see us reform. If anyone outside the band tries to push us back together, they might be well meaning, but I think it just makes it even more unlikely for anything at all to happen. Too many old bands take advantage of the public's good will by doing second rate "take the money and run" type gigs. The public, and any band members, would need to know that whoever was working together was doing it because they really wanted to, for genuine musical reasons, not just because someone was offering money or whatever. Otherwise I don't think it would be the real Specials. I put my name to the joint statement that there are no plans to reform in the foreseeable future, just like every other member from the original band did.

7.Lastly, talk is that 2 Tone should quite rightly be commemorated in someway in Coventry, I suggest a street named " 2 Tone Way". What would you like to see (if anything).

Renaming one of the multi storey car parks "Ghost Town Park" would do me, but seriously, if it's true anyone really wanted to do anything like your suggestion, it would be brilliant, it's not really for me to say though. Maybe because 2 Tone was against racism I should also really say I hope there's something in the city to commemorate people who've been killed in racist attacks, like Satnam Singh Gil who was twenty when he got killed in 1981. Doctor Amal Dharri got stabbed in the chip shop off Albany Rd. in the same year, it was supposedly for a fifty pence bet . I think they deserve to be remembered more than we do really.

I would like to thank Jerry for agreeing to do this interview for Backbeat ..good on ya Jerry! **Pete Chambers.**

85 C🌍VAID

STARRING

FOR EAST AFRICA

COLOURFIELD

WITH
DESTINY — EUROPEAN SUN
INTIMATE OBSESSIONS — JIMMY JIMMY — JUMPIN' BAD
MAJOR 5 — RED ON RED — SHEER PRIDE
SPIDER MURPHY — STILL LIFE — THIS HEAT
TERMINAL TEARS — 20 DAYS — SUPERNATURALS
WITH LOCAL SPORTING AND POLITICAL CELEBRITIES
AT THE

LANCHESTER POLYTECHNIC
STUDENT UNION PRIORY ST COVENTRY CV1 3FJ
SATURDAY OCTOBER 19th 1985

DOORS OPEN 5.30 p.m. TICKETS — £1 FOR
ADMISSION PLUS £4 DONATION
TICKETS AVAILABLE FROM COV. POLY STUDENTS
UNION. COVENTRY EVENING TELEGRAPH OFFICES,
COVENTRY INFORMATION AND MERCIA SOUND.
TELEPHONE ENQUIRIES COV. 618961 and 442607
(12.00 to 2.00 p.m.)

IN CONJUNCTION WITH MERCIA SOUND, BRUM BEAT,
COVENTRY EVENING TELEGRAPH, COV POLY S.U.
AND COVENTRY CABLE TV.

R.O.A.R.

Covaid raised £4.425 for African famine relief in 1985.

The Furious Apples
Coventry
Fronted by the tall enigmatic figure of Greg Crabb along with his brother Michael. They released the stunning single Engineering/Bella Donna in 1983.

Photos– top and bottom left the band on stage at The General Wolfe, below right Greg in 2006.

"We had this get up and do it yourself spirit in those days people just craved getting to together and start writing song in a punky anti-establishment way, but now I feel people in bands are striving to be part of the establishment and that's where it's all gone wrong". **Greg Crabb**

CBS Records were so interested in the Apples that they had them play their song Terminal Passion down the phone. A deal with CBS was lost when the Furious Apples loving A&R man left the company.

Alf Hardy was also part of large festival playing band Tubilah Dog, they had a political edge to them and would have probably been called Hippies had they surfaced two decades earlier. They became part of the fabled Hawkwind family and released records as Hawkdog.

Chris followed the album with a new very different project and stood for Parliament on behalf of Screaming Lord Sutch's Monster Party where he got to appear on TV's Newsnight with his Crocodile Tears album firmly in hand. "I stood for Matlock", reveals Chris, "The Newsnight interview was one of the shortest on record, they had just raised the deposit to £500 to stop the likes of me standing for Parliament so as soon as they saw the record under my arm they stopped filming pretty quickly. The party had some good ideas though, like getting everyone out of the country so we could give it a jolly good spring clean because the fabrics of society were becoming a bit eroded"! **Chris Sidwell**

Crocodile Tears
Coventry
Zany, madcap and off-the-wall, three words that just about sum up this band. Led for many years by Chris Sidwell, with more than a little help from Alf Hardy. As to be expected they have released a large body of work over the years, some of it now very collectable, they still continue to release CD's and play the 'odd' gig now and again.

Photos– above left the Crocs playing the Beer Engine 2007, top right Chris and Alf (on right) at Cabin Studios London Road, Coventry.

TWENTY RANDOM LOCAL SINGLES OF THE EIGHTIES IN NO PARTICULAR ORDER.

Everybody's Got a Mother (Badge)-Gods Toys (pic1)
Will You (A & M)-Hazel O'Connor
Let's Get Together (The Voyage International)-Steel Locks
Rat Race (2-Tone)-The Specials
Love & Pride (CBS)-King (pic 2)
Away/ Montovani (2-Tone)-The Swinging Cats
Thinking Of You (Chrysalis)-The Colourfield
Engineering (Sonar)-Furious Apples
General Public (IRS)-General Public
She Has Changed Not you (WEA)-Reluctant Stereotypes (pic 3)

On My Radio (2-Tone)-The Selecter (pic 4)
Go For It (Sky Blue)-Coventry City FC (pic 5)
Beauty Has Her Way (Geffen)-Mummy Calls
Revolving Boy (Cönsumer Disks)-Urge
Invisibility (Cherry Red)-Eyeless In Gaza
Plans For Today (WEA)-Reluctant Stereotypes
Move Into The Rhythm (Race Records)-Team 23
The Live EP (Too Much too Young) (2-Tone)-The Special AKA
Ghost Town (2-Tone)-The Specials (pic 6)
Send Me To Coventry (Halida)-The Mob

Eyeless In Gaza
Nuneaton
Electronic based duo (Martyn Bates and Pete Becker), they released a plethora of excellent albums for Cherry Red in the 80's. They reformed in 2005, and continued to produce intelligent atmospheric music.

Photos-Bottom and below Gaza (both pics Peter left, Martyn right) at The Wolfe.

Their first single Kodak Ghosts Run Amok is collectable it would set you back £25, if you could find it that is

Martyn was once the vocalist with the mark 1 Reluctant Stereotypes. Not something he is keen to talk about nowadays.

Their creativity was never caged by record company 'suits'. Pete Becker puts it like this "We were always pressuring the record company (Cherry Red). If we had struck a deal with a major, it would have been on acceptable terms as regards artistic content/presentation, so I guess they could have tried it on, but we would never do anything twice if we felt like fools the first time"! **Peter Becker**

Steve & Heather Taylor have also written songs for Shakin' Stevens and Irish heart-throb Daniel O'Donnell including his biggest hit Give A Little Love

Coventry City Football Club
Coventry
1987 was a good year for the Sky Blues, they won the FA Cup and got their campaign song Go For It in the charts to boot. Written by husband and wife song writing team Steve and Heather Taylor, it was the soundtrack to that glorious time in the City's history.

Photos-Above CCFC on Blue Peter, below left Steve & Heather 2005, below right the team recording at the couples house in 87.

"The record, released (of course) on the Sky Blue label spent two weeks in the Top 100, making it to number 61, whereas opponents Spurs' record that year reached the Top Twenty, getting to number 18. I had risen to the heady heights of Managing Director and Programme Controller at Mercia by that time, and I decreed that not only would we not play the Spurs record, but that we would play "Go For It!" as often as a Top 10 record - on very high rotation. Needless to say it was Number 1 on Mercia's own chart by the time the Cup Final came round". **Stuart Linnell**

Hot Snax
Coventry

Madcap inventive band, originally called The Machine (as featured on The Sent From Coventry LP with Character Change). Members have included former Specials drummer Silverton and the zany Roland 'Ollie' Oliver or Doc Mustard in their ranks as well as Michael Collins, Julian Bell, Jim Pryal and Tony Clarke. They supported ska band Bad Manners in 1982.

Photos– Below The Machine, with Ollie far left, Bottom Hot Snax.

Hot Snax once came first in a Mercia Sound Music Competition.

"I have indelible memories of listening to my parents collection of 78's on the walnut radiogram. From the Blues Of The Night to The Warsaw Concerto. I was packed off to boarding School in Gt Crosby, Liverpool. Overall it was quite a traumatic experience which is why I left of my own accord aged sixteen rather than get expelled for smoking pot and mourning the era of the Beatles which was an intense influence during my incarceration in Liverpool. The boarding school was an environment of fear and longing. During the first years TV was denied and so music was the only escape". **Ollie**

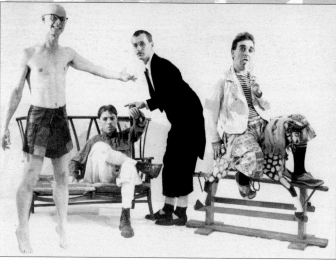

Criminal Class
Coventry
Skinhead band fronted by Craig St Leon, they rejected the usual right-wing leanings most Oi/Skin bands held (that didn't stop them being lumped in with them though). Oi guru Gary Bushell was a fan and it led to them appearing on the controversial compilation album Strength through Oi
Photos– right an original line-up of the band, below the 2002 version and bottom Craig St Leon 2007.

The band influenced American band Criminal Class USA, who are still rocking today.

The band continues to play today, now with former Squad front man Gus Chambers on vocals.

The TV news programme Nationwide got into the act, and did a piece on the skinhead Oi movement, and read out Criminal Class's lyrics to Blood on The Streets claiming them racist. "Gary Bushell defended us" Craig reveals, " What it was we sang White youth, but in the next verse we sang black youth, it was about the race riots, but it was all taken out of context and twisted, the truth was I had a muslim girlfriend at the time, so how could I be racist?". **Craig St Leon**

Hazel O'Connor
Coventry

Hit huge with the film Breaking Glass, and was immediately christened the Queen of Punk. She hit the charts on many occasions, though it was the songs D-Days, Eighth Day and Will You that made the biggest impact. She continues to act and sing.

Photos-above left, both of Hazel at the Butts 1981, above right, Hazel at The Fletch 2007.

She appeared on ITV's show Hit Me Baby One More Time. Performing her classic Will You and a stunningly original take on Kylie Minogue's Can't Get It Out Of My Head. She sadly didn't win (losing out to Hue & Cry) I talked to her on the eve of the show she was excited by the whole experience." I'm just happy to be here, win or lose it doesn't matter, I'm just happy having this opportunity". I asked her if she had the chance would she do the whole Breaking Glass thing again and she replied, "! I would absolutely do it all again, definitely".
Hazel O'Connor.

Hazel's first TV appearance was on kid's TV show Metal Mickey as female robot Roberta.

Hazel took part in the all day charity concert held at the Butts Stadium in 1981 My personal stand out moment was towards the end of Hazel O'Connor's set, she came and sat down her legs dangling over the front of the stage. The opening bars of Will You began and the words spine and shivers spring to mind. A beautiful song, a beautiful moment and the end to a terrific day.

The Pink Umbrellas
Coventry

Half of the Reluctant Stereotypes went off to be King the other half became the Pink Umbrellas. Paul Sampson and Steve Edgson were later joined by Rob Hill and Barry Jones. They created the conceptual psychedelic show based around The Toy Museum and Joseph Monk. Sadly the only track that ever saw the light of day was Raspberry Rainbow. Ready Steady Go Records released it as a single, although it never charted it did however pick up a lot of radio play.

Photos– Above left Paul (on left) and Steve in an early publicity shot I took at the Wolfe, above right Steve at the Wolfe, Below Paul at the Wolfe, spot the stage props.

Their one and only single Raspberry Rainbow now demands a £20 price tag for a mint copy.

"We wanted to do something fun again Paul and myself had similar tastes in music with bands like early Pink Floyd and The Soft Machine. We came up with a concept idea of a rather strange man named Joseph Monk who ran a Toy Museum. We used lots of cut-outs on stage we had a commentary between songs, but it just got too elaborate for a band of our stature, had we the money I think it would have worked rather well".
Steve Edgson

91

The Human Cabbages

Coventry

Steve Teers was the creative force behind the band, they favoured female vocalists and appeared on the Coventry Compilation EP Boys and Girls Come Out To play.

Photos– Below left a one-off reformed Cabbages, below right, Stan and Whiff, bottom an original line-up of the Cabbages in full swing.

"It was about this time that we were approached by Guy Surtees from a band called Profile about putting together a Compilation EP. He also put an ad in Alternative Sounds and after a meeting, the idea for 'Boys and Girls Come Out To Play' was formed. The pink side was fronted by female singers, the blue by males. No big financial music mogul's around though - each band had to fork out about a hundred quid to make it happen. Whilst others booked the recording time at Woodbine, Leamington, I took on board the printing of the vinyl & the covers. The bands came up with there own artwork which made up with a sixth of the sleeve wrap & it took a few calls to Sounds music paper to dig up the numbers of mastering & duplication factories. MySpace was a long way off then".

Steve Teers

The Boys and Girls Come Out To Play EP, now commands high prices from collectors. It came with a pink side for girls and a blue for boys and a natty fold out poster sleeve.

Chris Dickie once shared a flat with Specials mainman Jerry Dammers

Chris became an engineer and has worked with the likes of Depeche Mode, The Pogues and Morrissey. He now lives in Australia.

Gods Toys
Coventry
If you want a band that summed up Coventry's musical reinvention of the 80's, then Gods Toys were it. Loud, proud and oh so original. All The Born Losers and Everybody's Got A Mother, were the bands two changeling singles. Dill and the boys should have been huge, but despite great reviews in the national music press, they sadly never fulfilled their initial promise.

Photos-Gods Toys photos are very scarce so getting two is pretty good going.

"We got together when Chris Dickie and I met Nick through Jerome Heisler (The End)", Dill explains, "and I recruited Larry from college and finally John Hobley joined us on drums three gigs into our creation, that was all back in 1978 and the Lord said let there be weirdness and so it came to pass". "Our first gig was Battle of the Bands at Warwick University, but we unfairly came 2nd in the final- (X certs Payola scam) ha ha...! We supported The Specials on our third gig organised through Horace Panter ...a judge for the previous competition". **Dill**

Team 23
Coventry

Cov's funk soul brothers, represented blue eyed soul not dissimilar to the Dexys Midnight Runners brand. The changing line-up included names like Jerome Heisler, Mick Galic (who actually became a Dexy's), Dave Pepper, John Hewitt, and Jim Lantsbery who both would later join King. They signed a deal to John Bradbury's Race Record and released the rather good Move into the Rhythm single.

Photos, top Team 23 Mrk 2 with John Hewitt far left Jerome with scarf, and Jim Lantsbery second right. Bottom, Team 23 Mrk 1, with Dave Pepper first left.
Insert the great John Hewitt circa 2006, still looking cool.

"Basically for the last five months of the band. We spent all of the time rehearsing and we only ever played one night with that line-up, actually at The Sportsman's Arms. During all this I had auditioned for Dexy's Midnight Runners, and actually got the job, so by the time we played the last gig, we all knew it was over for Team 23. My lasting memory of the band was the enthusiasm and skill we all had, even at that young age, we had a lot of promise and potential that was never realized". **Mick Galic**

An aborted EP would have included the following live tracks recorded in Norwich. Body & Soul, Hold On I'm Coming, End Of The Line, Touch Me and What's the Game.

Reluctant Stereotypes
Coventry

Yet another local 80's band that looked set for big things. Began as a jazz-rock set up then adopted the Coventry ska sound and signed with WEA Records. They released a batch of above average singles and one great album entitled The Label. Paul King, Colin Heanes and Tony Wall would later form King. While Steve Edgson and Paul Sampson would form The Pink Umbrellas.

Photos–Above, Tony, Paul Sampson, Paul King, Steve Edgson and Colin Heanes. Right Steve (top) and Paul Sampson 2005. Below Paul King and Steve on stage at the Butts gig.

"The Reluctant Stereotypes was Horizon Studios house band which is where my music career began. We toured the nations clubs; pubs & universities for two years non-stop finally claiming a performance in the Old Grey Whistle Test alongside Adam & the Ants as they banged Ant mania onto the pop charts". **Paul King**

Paul Sampson would go on to produce The Primitives and Catatonia among others.

The 1981 Reading Festival featured (along with The Reluctant Stereotypes) the following bands; The Kinks, Greg Lake, Wishbone Ash and The Enid

95

The Selecter
Coventry

The Selecter did it their way, compare them with the Specials at your own peril. Neol Davies's insightful and danceable songs were the perfect ammunition for Pauline Black's acerbic deliveries. When this band were hot, they were hot, and probably represented the Two Tone ethos better than any of the other bands on the label. Classics like Too Much Pressure, On my Radio and Three Minute Hero will still call you to the dance floor whenever they are played.

Photos– Top & bottom right rare shots of Pauline and Neol finally back together on stage in 2007 at Anthony Harty's 40th. Plus a standard shot of the band.

Despite the fact that they will forever be labelled a Two tone band, they actually left the label as early as 1980.

"The Selecter was life-changing for both the band members and the fantastic audiences we played for, changes still reverberating even now, nearly 30 years on. The 2 Tone movement was perhaps the last of the music/fashion movements and some would regret the fact that these events will never happen again in the same way or have the same substance. Never mind, we rocked...and that's the main thing". **Neol Davies**

THE GENERAL WOLFE

THE Nº 1 VENUE FOR LIVE BANDS & DISCO
ROCK & ROLL ON SATURDAY NIGHTS
WED. THURSDAY FRIDAY. SATURDAY 12·00 BARS

GIG GUIDE

APRIL

THURSDAY 9TH	RELUCTANT STEREOTYPES
FRIDAY 10TH	MUSIC FOR PLEASURE + CHANNEL A
SATURDAY 11TH	DYNAMITE
THURSDAY 16TH	THE STREETWALKERS + L'HOMME DE TERRE
SATURDAY 18TH	ROCK 'N' ROLL & ROCKABILLY DISCO
EASTER MONDAY	CLASSIFIED (ROCK BAND)
THURSDAY 23RD	I
FRIDAY 24TH	GROOVY LEPERS
SATURDAY 25TH	THE STEVE GIBBONS BAND
THURSDAY 30TH	DEDYAMPY + AXIOM BRANCHES + THIN SERG

MAY

FRIDAY 1ST	BRIGHT EYES + VIXEN (2 ROCK BANDS)
SATURDAY 2ND	ROCK 'N' ROLL & ROCKABILLY DISCO
WEDNESDAY 6TH	WILD BOYS
THURSDAY 7TH	SMALL CHANGE
FRIDAY 8TH	FLAT BACKERS + CHANNEL A
SATURDAY 9TH	CRAZY CAVAN & THE RYTHAM ROCKERS
WEDNESDAY 13TH	SPOILED NEGATIVES + FLACK OFF
THURSDAY 14TH	I
FRIDAY 15TH	CHANNEL A + ROUGH-BEATS
SATURDAY 16TH	ROCK 'N' ROLL & ROCKABILLY DISCO
WEDNESDAY 20TH	SNEAK PREVIEW (ROCK BAND)
THURSDAY 21ST	SINATRAS + KITKATS
FRIDAY 22ND	MOSQUITO'S + DTS (R&B)
SATURDAY 23RD	JETS
THURSDAY 28TH	GRACE (ROCK BAND)
FRIDAY 29TH	SNEAKY PIERRE. CURRENT MEMBERS OF 10cc, SAD CAFE & REAL THING

JUNE

| FRIDAY 5TH | THE ERIC BELL BAND |

WATCH OUT FOR THE GIG GUIDES

A General Wolfe Gig Guide flyer from 1981, gigs I would have gone to have included The Reluctant Stereotypes, "I" and The Wild Boys, all great nights out!

Quiz time, who would live in a house like this?
Just a bit of fun, but can you link the local
Musical stars with the Coventry homes they lived in?

EVENLODE CRESCENT

KINGSWAY

HEN LANE

1

2

3

BURLINGTON RD

4

5

WYKEN AVE

6

7

8

BRAMBLE ST

HEN LANE

ALBANY ROAD

To help you here are the people who lived in the houses opposite, can you match them up answers at the bottom of page 100.

HAZEL O'CONNOR

PETE WATERMAN

VINCE HILL

ROB WOODWARD

HORACE PANTER

FRANK IFIELD

JERRY DAMMERS

BOB BROLLY

You can read Pete's Backbeat column in the

Coventry Telegraph

every Tuesday

http://iccoventry.icnetwork.co.uk/nostalgia/backbeat/

and
hear Pete's **Backtracking** segment on the Bob Brolly Show, every Friday from 3.00 pm on

BBC Coventry & Warwickshire

On **94.8FM, 104FM, 103.7FM**
and DAB Digital Radio
and streamed online at
www.bbc.co.uk/coventry

Quiz Time Answers – House 1= Frank Ifield, House 2=Rob Woodward, House 3= Vince Hill, House 4= Pete Waterman, House 5=Hazel O'Connor, House 6= Horace Panter, House 7= Bob Brolly, House 8= Jerry Dammers.

VINTAGE TACKLE

Offering customers reasonably priced, modern new fishing tackle also good quality used items. There is also a large selection of ground bait and frozen bait available. We also buy used tackle or part exchange on new items.

For further information contact Ron on 07816936352 or e-mail ron.farmer@ntlworld.com

COVENTRY MARKET
STALL 95

In addition we cater for the traditional angler with a range of vintage reels, rods and traditional hand made floats. A small deposit will secure items for one month. Fishing related items always wanted, e.g. books, china etc.

Coventry Myton Hospice Appeal
The campaign to build a new hospice in Coventry

Myton Hamlet Hospice is a registered charity (508768) and was established in 1979 by a group headed by the then Bishop of Coventry, Rt. Rev. John Gibbs. Their vision of providing specialist palliative care for the people of Warwickshire and Coventry was realised when the hospice was opened in 1982 at a location in the heart of Warwickshire, close to the town centres of Warwick and Leamington Spa. The campaign continues to see a new Myton Hospital in Coventry.

Donations are very much welcome
Please contact...

Myton Hamlet Hospice
Myton Road
Warwick
CV34 6PX

Telephone 01926 838818
or 02476 411177
Fax 01926 409110
Email coventry.appeal@mytonhospice.org

-This advert is in loving memory of-
-Helen Beard-

GROVEWOOD

THE DOG & TRUMPET
HERTFORD STREET COVENTRY

Welcome to the famous Dog & Trumpet

Coventry's Number one underground nightclub

Live bands every Saturday night

Drinks promotions

Alternative nights with Indi, Rock, Punk, Emo, Ska, Dance and Cheese

Students Welcome

WE MAY LIVE IN A MUSEUM..... BUT THAT DOESN'T MEAN OUR EQUIPMENT BELONGS IN ONE!

Herbert Recording Studio

Coventry city centre's modern professional multitrack digital recording studio. Record in-house with our engineers from **£15 p/h** (**£10 concession**) or, if you like, we'll teach you how to engineer it for yourself.

HERBERT MEDIA
The Herbert, Jordan Well, Coventry CV1 5QP
T: 02476 832310 / **E:** info@herbertmedia.org
W: www.herbertmedia.org
M: www.myspace.com/herbertmedia_audio

RENAISSANCE
WEST MIDLANDS

Coventry City Council